A gift to

From

THANKS DAD!

LESSONS FROM THE LAKE
—ON LIVING AND LOVING

Penelope J. Stokes

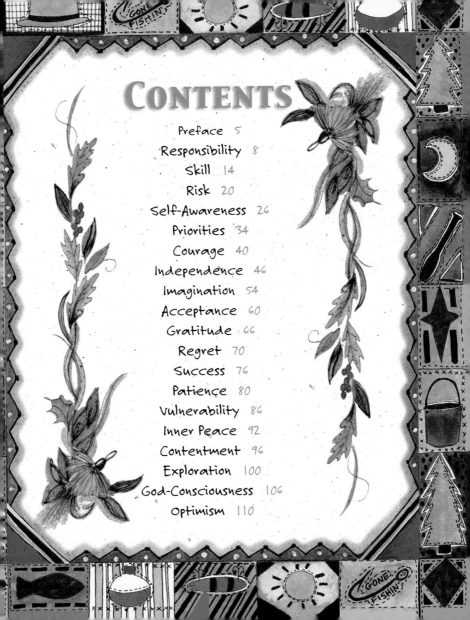

CONTENTS

Preface 5

Responsibility 8

Skill 14

Risk 20

Self-Awareness 26

Priorities 34

Courage 40

Independence 46

Imagination 54

Acceptance 60

Gratitude 66

Regret 70

Success 76

Patience 80

Vulnerability 86

Inner Peace 92

Contentment 96

Exploration 100

God-Consciousness 106

Optimism 110

PREFACE

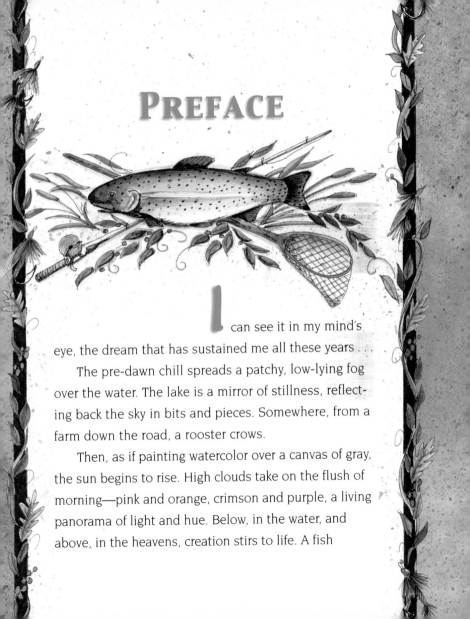

I can see it in my mind's eye, the dream that has sustained me all these years . . .

The pre-dawn chill spreads a patchy, low-lying fog over the water. The lake is a mirror of stillness, reflecting back the sky in bits and pieces. Somewhere, from a farm down the road, a rooster crows.

Then, as if painting watercolor over a canvas of gray, the sun begins to rise. High clouds take on the flush of morning—pink and orange, crimson and purple, a living panorama of light and hue. Below, in the water, and above, in the heavens, creation stirs to life. A fish

jumps, scattering droplets of water like multi-colored gemstones; a bird calls, rousing a chorus of replies.

Like a gong struck deep within my soul, my whole heart resonates with the sight and sound, the smell and taste and touch. And the memories come flooding back.

Not one memory, but a hundred, a thousand. All the principles I learned without even knowing I was being taught.

They are with me today, those lessons from the lake, woven inextricably into the fabric of my life. They've taught me how to laugh and cry, how to be vulnerable and tough, how to discover and draw upon the deep inner resources of my soul. They've given me the power to overcome disappointment and heartache, the backbone to stand up for my convictions, the wisdom to know when to let go. They've pointed me in the right direction, led me to a place of wonder and glory where risk is an adventure and the future is bright with promises.

These are my lessons from the lake.

My inheritance.

My father's legacy.

Penelope J. Stokes
April, 2000

7

Give a girl a fish, and you feed her for a day.

Teach a girl to fish, and you feed her for a lifetime.

ADAPTED FROM A CHINESE PROVERB

RESPONSIBILITY

"Bait your own hook; clean your own catch."

When I was a little girl, perhaps nine or ten, my dad purchased a lot on a private lake some twelve miles out of town. There was nothing there until many years later, not even a boathouse. Just a dock, a single water pipe, and (my mother's contribution) an old porch swing suspended from a couple of tall oak trees.

Every Saturday before dawn my father loaded up his little fishing boat, made a quick stop at the bait shop for coffee and crickets, and returned home in the early afternoon with a stringer full of bass and bream.

I was fascinated by this weekly ritual, adhered to as religiously as the Sunday morning scramble to get everyone ready for church on time. Finally, one Saturday evening, as he dipped a small bass filet into his special batter and placed it in the sizzling skillet, Daddy turned to me and asked, "Want to go fishing with me next weekend?"

I was elated. I had always been Daddy's girl, and nothing I could dream of compared with the prospect of spending a whole Saturday morning with him. "But if you go, " he warned sternly, "you'll have to get up early. And you'll have to bait your own hook and clean your own catch. No daughter of mine is going to be pampered in my boat."

I didn't want to be pampered. I wanted to learn how to fish. I wanted him to be proud of me. And so the following Saturday morning, I rolled out of bed while it was still dark, threw on an old pair of jeans

Pinecone Lodge

and a sweatshirt, and met him in the kitchen while he was still stirring sugar into his first cup of coffee.

We didn't talk much on the drive out to the lake. We just sat in the truck and watched the scenery bounce by.

"Remember what I told you?" he asked as he handed me a life jacket and held the boat steady for me to climb in.

"Yes, sir. I have to bait my own hook and clean my own catch."

He nodded, started the outboard motor, and we were off.

He used a rod and reel. I used a cane pole with a big red bobber, and felt a little like Opie Taylor. "You do it like this," he instructed, reaching into the cricket box and deftly threading the bait onto the hook. "Now you try it."

Daddy didn't do much fishing that day. He wet his line a little, and came up with a few strikes, but mostly he watched me, grinning from ear to ear, as I fell in love with the sport he enjoyed so much. At noon we made for shore and cleaned our catch on a board

11

hammered into a makeshift table between two trees. He showed me how to hold the fish by the gills, scrape the scales off, and leave the heads and entrails for the homeless cats that prowled around the lake in search of food. I scraped most of the skin off my knuckles before I got the hang of it, my jeans and sweatshirt were filthy, and my pony tail was filled with scales, but I couldn't have been happier.

Mother met us at the door, turning up her nose at the smell but admiring the fish dripping on the carport floor.

"She caught most of them," my dad said in an unmistakable tone of pride. "And she did it by herself, too. I'm going to have to keep an eye on this one if I don't want to lose my title as Master of the Lake." He put a hand on my shoulder and squeezed gently. "Yeah, you outdid me this time, but how about a rematch next week?" he asked. "I've got a reputation to protect, after all."

My heart soared. Daddy was proud of me!

I had baited my own hook (well, most of the time) and cleaned my own catch (sort of). And it was only the beginning . . .

12

Daddy didn't do much fishing that day.
He wet his line a little, and came up with
a few strikes, but mostly he watched me,
grinning from ear to ear, as I fell in love
with the sport he enjoyed so much.

It didn't take long for me to graduate from a cane pole and bright red bobber to a rod and reel like the one Dad used. As a child I was pretty athletic, playing tennis and volleyball and—when the boys would let me—sand-lot baseball. My hand-eye coordination was good, and I had been watching Daddy cast out and reel in. I was sure I could do it.

"Okay," he said, handing over the rod. "Put your thumb there, on the release button, then let go when you throw your line out."

I took the rod and positioned it in my right hand. This was going to be great. I intended to show him a cast the likes of which he'd never seen before. And then, with an enormous effort, I raised the rod over my head and heaved it as if I were slamming an overhead volley down my opponent's throat.

The tip of the rod hit the side of the boat, and the line dropped into the water two feet away with a pathetic, gurgling sound. Not exactly a moment of glory.

15

I stared at the line. Something was attached to the hook, floating on the surface of the lake. It was my father's fishing hat.

Embarrassed, I turned to look at him. He was rubbing his ear, wiping blood from a small cut at the top of his earlobe. I reeled in the line and handed him his dripping hat. And as much as I wanted to know what I had done wrong, I couldn't bring myself to ask.

"Unless you're planning to use my eyeball as bait, go a little easier next time," he said. "It's finesse, not

force. It doesn't take a lot of effort. Snap it out from the wrist, like this." He lifted his rod and, barely moving his arm, sent his own line arching out toward the shoreline. The bait plummeted down perfectly between a rock and a submerged tree. "See? No big splash, just a quiet little plop."

I resumed my place in the front of the boat and tried again. This time I didn't inflict any physical wounds, but I did get my line tangled in the branches of a tree. I hooked a rock. I caught the anchor rope. Just as I thought I was getting the hang of it, I watched as my line went in one direction and my bait flew off in another. Meanwhile, Dad was catching anything that moved, and the fish basket was filling up.

Tired and frustrated, I reeled in, re-baited my hook, and sat there for a minute. My whole arm ached, my head throbbed, and I was on the verge of tears. I bit my lip and half-heartedly flipped a side-armed cast out into the water.

Much to my surprise, the line spun out gracefully, in a shallow arc, and sailed with near-perfection into a small quiet pool near the shore. "Nice cast," Dad commented, his eyes still fixed on his own line.

I reeled in a little, waited, then began to reel again. A fat bluegill clamped down on the bait and began to run with it. My joy returned, and the thrill of playing that fish rushed through me. More importantly, I had, in my weariness, stumbled upon the technique Dad had been trying to teach me.

How many times, I wonder, have I tried to strong-arm my

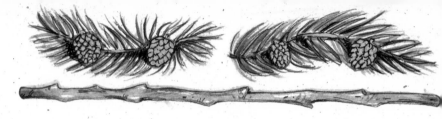

I discovered a different kind of pleasure—
the satisfaction that comes with doing
something simple, and doing it well.

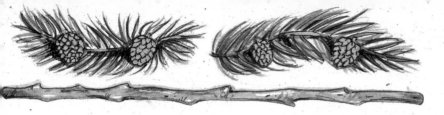

way into success—to deliver a power blow, to use brawn and brute determination rather than skill and quiet confidence? And all the time, the principle was right there in front of me: Not force, but finesse. The secret is in the motion, not the muscle.

I did not, of course, master all the skills I needed in that first day of learning to cast. I still got hung up on tree limbs and rocks from time to time, but the more I practiced, the more it became second nature to me—that flick of the wrist, that little hesitation just before the line spins out. And I discovered a different kind of pleasure—the satisfaction that comes with doing something simple, and doing it well.

A little skill, a little restraint. Confidence, not coercion.

No big splash, just a quiet little plop.

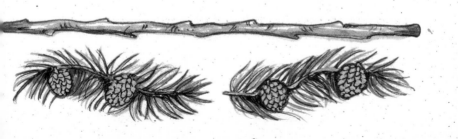

RISK

"The big one waits in the weeds."

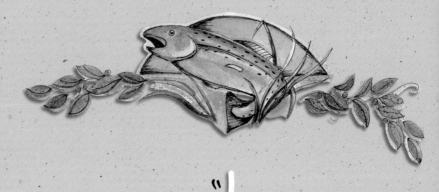

"I once hooked into a big bass over there," Daddy said, pointing toward the shore where a tangle of weeds rose above the surface. "Biggest one I'd ever seen—the great-granddaddy of all bass." He nodded in my direction. "Throw your line in there. Maybe you'll catch him."

I had my doubts. If my father couldn't catch him, I was pretty sure nobody could—especially not a novice

like me. But I didn't say that. Like an obedient daughter, I cast into the spot and began to reel in. A split second later, a heavy weight snapped the line taut.

"I got him! I got him!" I yelled, forgetting that I was supposed to be quiet. I held my breath, pulled the rod tip up as I had been taught, and reeled furiously, certain that at any moment the enormous fish would break the water in a glorious lunge.

Dad sat back and watched, smiling. After a minute or two he reached down, grabbed my line with one hand, and lifted a dripping wad of seaweed out of the lake. "Well," he said with a chuckle, "at least we'll have salad for dinner tonight."

The bait was gone, and the hook was bent. But he wouldn't let me quit. He straightened the hook with a pair of pliers, and I put on fresh bait. "Try again."

"In the same place?" I protested. "There's nothing but weeds over there."

He shrugged, pointing toward clearer water. "You can cast out further, where you won't get hung up. But the big one waits in the weeds."

With a longsuffering sigh, I tried again. Twice.

21

Three times. With every cast, the result was the same.
My line snagged every imaginable variety of underwater
plant. Frustrated and depressed, I was ready to give up.
This was nothing more than an exercise in futility,
designed either to test the limits of my temper or to
give Dad a good laugh at my expense. Then, on what
seemed like the hundredth cast into the weed bed, I
felt a tug. Not the steady, heavy pull of waterlogged
seaweed, but a living movement at the end of my line.

I jerked the rod to set the hook, but kept my lips
clamped firmly together. I wasn't about to say a word,
not until I saw for myself that I had hooked the entree,
and not a side order of slimy vegetables.

I felt the line move from one side to the other. Felt
the rush of adrenaline as the tension slacked off a little,

then tightened when the fish began its dive. I played him, just the way Daddy had shown me, giving him a bit of room to run, then reeling him closer and closer to the boat. My rod tip bent, jumping furiously with the movement of the fish. And then I saw him, a flash of silver coming toward the light. With a mighty lunge he broke the surface, scattering beads of water in the morning sun.

Not a giant. Not one you'd hang on the wall. Not the great-granddaddy of all bass, but a nice, respectable catch.

"He's a keeper, I'd say." Daddy put the landing net under him and lifted him into the boat, then held the bass up for me to admire. "See? What did I tell you?"

I nodded. "The big one waits in the weeds."

"Yep. You might get tangled up a little, and maybe you'll even feel like a fool. But if you don't take the risk, you never catch 'em."

I knew it was true. All my frustration, all that time fussing with the weeds, had been worth it. That bass had been down there the whole time, waiting. I just had to take the risk to catch him. A dozen risks. A

**FISHY FISHY IN THE BROOK
PAPA CATCH HIM ON A HOOK
MOMMA FRY HIM IN A PAN
BABY EAT HIM LIKE A MAN**

hundred. I might have felt like an incompetent idiot, but if I had given up, I never would have seen him break into the sunlight in all his power and glory.

Much of what we want out of life lies waiting in the weeds. The hopes, the plans, the dreams. But nothing worthwhile comes easily. The risk, the frustration, the challenge are all part of the process. Lost bait, broken lines, bent hooks.

Still, it's down there, hiding in the darkness.

The Big Dream, waiting among the weeds.

You've just got to keep casting.

Nothing worthwhile comes easily.

The risk, the frustration, the challenge

are all part of the process.

One Saturday morning, when I was about twelve, Dad pushed the boat offshore, revved up the engine, and then turned to me. "Come back here," he said. "You're going to drive today."

With me at the motor and Dad on the second seat, we began to make our way out of the cove into the middle of the lake. It was confusing at first, not at all like steering my bicycle, where I turned the wheel in the direction I wanted to go. With an outboard, everything was backward—I had to shift the handle right to go left. But after a few wobbly moments, we were off, roaring down the lake with the wind in our hair.

Along the way, Dad pointed out landmarks—the house on the north shore, the narrow, finger-shaped cove to the east. A white boathouse on the left, a red one on the right. The weed bed where I caught my first bass. But I didn't pay too much attention. I was caught up in the thrill of driving the boat for the first time.

We eased into a small inlet bordered by a stand of willows, dropped anchor, and began to fish. I caught several bluegills, and Daddy hooked into a nice-sized bass. After a while we moved to another spot, a wide bay flanked with rocks and pine trees. In a couple of hours we had a good mess of fish for dinner. The morning fog had burned off, and the sun had climbed high into the sky.

"It's nearly noon," Dad said, squinting overhead. "You about ready to head in?"

"I guess so."

He pulled the anchor into the boat and pointed at

the engine. "Push the primer a couple of times, then crank her up."

I pulled on the rope, and after a few tugs the outboard motor chugged to life. With the throttle in my hand, I sat back and looked at him. "Which way?"

He grinned and lifted one eyebrow. "You brought us out here; you take us in."

I looked around, and a sense of panic washed over me. I had no idea which way to go. Everything looked the same—the rocks, the shoreline, the trees. Even the sun gave me no help —at high noon, I couldn't tell which way was east and which was west.

At last my father rescued me from my dilemma. "Head out that direction." He pointed. "And this time, keep

28

your eye on the landmarks."

We made our way back, keeping close to the shoreline and moving slowly. After a while a boathouse came into view—the red one, which I was sure should have been on the other side of the lake. I relaxed a little when we passed the weed bed, and breathed a sigh of relief when the house on the north shore appeared. I was home free.

"Now, where's our lot?" he prompted.

I pointed straight ahead and to the right. "Over there, I think." I steered the boat in that direction, but saw nothing that looked even vaguely familiar. We rounded a bend and kept going, and all the time I was searching the shoreline for the familiar sight of our little docking spot and the two big pine trees that marked the perimeter of our property.

Dad let me go on for a while longer, until I threw the engine into idle and turned to him. "I don't know," I confessed, feeling a little ashamed.

He pointed behind me. "Look around."

I scanned every inch of visible shoreline. At last I saw it, nearly hidden on a hillside up in the trees. The

There is nothing
half so much worth doing
as simply messing
about in boats

K. Grahame

weekend cabin that belonged to Lola, a family friend. It looked very different from this direction, but if it was indeed her house, I knew where I was. "Is that Lola's place?"

He nodded. "Don't feel too bad. It's easy to get lost unless you keep an eye on your landmarks."

I steered the boat toward the cove where Lola's house sat, then inched down the shoreline until I came to our lot. We pulled the boat in, cleaned our fish, and headed home. Dad didn't mention to Mother or anyone else that I had gotten lost on the lake, nor did he ever bring it up again. And from that time forward, I always kept a lookout for the landmarks that would lead me back.

I hadn't really been in any danger, of course. My father was in the boat, and he knew the way. But by letting me get lost, he taught me a lesson that has served me well throughout my life—*keep an eye on your landmarks.*

Life is full of twists and turns; bearing changes, hidden coves. And if we don't learn the value of self-awareness, we can easily be lured away from ourselves,

31

from the principles and values that make us who we are.

It's not difficult to get off track. Obvious temptations like money, success, prestige, or power can divert us from our course. But even subtler "lures"—conformity, belonging, affirmation, or love—can lead us away from fundamental principles like honor and integrity, justice and truth, faithfulness and commitment. These are our fixed points, signals of the soul that keep us on an even keel with ourselves, with God, and with those we love.

These are the landmarks that will guide us safely home.

Honor and integrity, justice and truth,
faithfulness and commitment. These are
our fixed points, signals of the soul that keep
us on an even keel with ourselves, with
God, and with those we love.

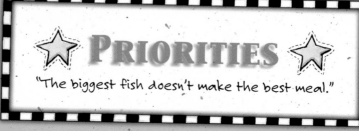

PRIORITIES

"The biggest fish doesn't make the best meal."

Dad and I didn't always talk a lot when we were in the boat together. Sometimes we'd fish all morning without exchanging more than a few words. It was enough to be together, to watch the sun rise, to sit in a quiet cove and listen to the sounds of nature around us.

One morning, however, I could tell there was something on Daddy's mind. He seemed distracted,

far away. He kept staring off into the distance, as if seeing something he wasn't sure he understood. But I couldn't ask him what was bothering him. I was only eleven or twelve at the time, and I didn't think I had a right to pry.

I waited. He thought. Then, finally, he said, "I've been offered a promotion at work."

A surge of pleasure went through me. I had always been proud of what my father did for a living. He was a social worker, and in his current job he worked for the Veteran's Administration, enabling veterans and their families to get the benefits they were entitled to. He helped people. He was good at it, and he was passionate about it. But as I watched his face, I realized he had misgivings about this new offer.

"Your mother and I decided we needed to talk to you kids about it," he went on. "It's an administrative position. More status, more prestige. A big raise, a lot more money coming in." He hesitated. "But we'd have to relocate . . . to Washington, D.C."

I closed my eyes and fought back tears. I wanted my dad to be successful, and the promotion was a big

35

step up. But I didn't want to move. I didn't want to
leave my friends and go to a big, noisy city where I didn't
know a soul. Still, I knew in my heart there wasn't a
thing I could do about it.

"So what do you think?" he asked.

I shrugged and tried to smile. Why was he asking me?
"I don't know. It . . . it sounds like a good opportunity,
I guess."

"It is," he agreed. "But I think my answer is going to
be no."

My jaw dropped open. "You're not going to take
it?"

He cast his line into the water and reeled it
back toward the boat. "Sometimes the
high-profile job with the
huge paycheck isn't
the right choice."
He paused for a
minute and then
went on. "I love
my work. I'm
happy doing

36

what I'm doing, and I'm not sure I'd like being an administrator. Besides, the only real reason to consider it is the raise, and I'm not sure it's ever a good idea to make a big life decision solely on the basis of money."

Dad gazed at me intently. "You only get one chance at life, honey, so you've got to be careful what you fish for. The biggest catch doesn't always make the best meal."

Our society tells us otherwise—loudly, and with increasing frequency. Happiness can be bought for the price of a winning lottery ticket. Money is the answer to life's problems and pressures. More is better. Go after the gold with everything you've got.

Most of us ordinary folks, I suppose, long for some measure of financial stability. But beyond the basics such as food, shelter, and transportation, what do we really need? Love, commitment, a sense of belonging. A community of supportive family and friends. Meaningful work. Dreams and visions and hope for the future. Wisdom. A spiritual awareness that sustains and feeds the soul.

Can these gifts be bought? No. Not with a gold card . . . not with stock liquidations . . . not with status or prestige or financial success.

The priority is not wealth but the intangible riches that come to a liberated soul.

Be careful what you fish for.

38

The priority is not wealth, but the intangible riches that come to a liberated soul.

COURAGE

"To find the fish, you have to get out of the cove."

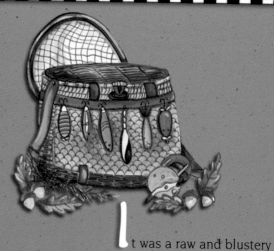

It was a raw and blustery autumn morning, with low clouds overhanging the water. Inside the perimeter of our little cove, the water seemed calm enough, reflecting back the gray of the sky. But out in the middle of the lake, the wind whipped the surface into whitecaps.

Daddy filled up the gas can, started the motor, and took us out. "Put on your life jacket," he yelled over the noise of wind and engine.

I shivered and pulled my sweatshirt and life vest closer, but a cold bead of fear ran down my spine. The lake was rough—rougher than I had ever seen it.

"Do you think we should go out in this?"

He laughed. "We'll be all right. Hold on tight, now. Here we go."

We made our way across the lake, buffeted by wind and water, and finally took refuge in a protected inlet on the other side. There the fish were biting fairly well—at least well enough to justify the trip.

Dad didn't seem the least bit disconcerted by the weather. He shared his coffee, laughed and talked a little, and after a few minutes hooked into a really nice bass. I caught a few, but my heart wasn't in it. Every time I looked behind me, I could see those waves out in the middle of the lake, taunting me, reminding me

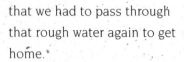

42

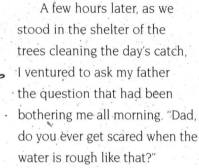

that we had to pass through that rough water again to get home.

A few hours later, as we stood in the shelter of the trees cleaning the day's catch, I ventured to ask my father the question that had been bothering me all morning. "Dad, do you ever get scared when the water is rough like that?"

He looked down at me. "Were you scared this morning?"

"A little," I admitted. "I kept thinking about all the times you come out here and fish alone. What if something happened to you?"

He laid his scaling knife on the table and gave me his full attention. "Your old daddy's no fool, honey. It's what we call an

Courage

THE TROUT DOCK

acceptable risk. If the weather's too bad, I don't go out.
But sometimes you have to take chances. It may be
calmer here in our little cove, but to find the fish,
you've got to get out of the cove."

43

He held up the big bass and grinned. "If we hadn't
taken the gamble, we never would have caught this
fellow, would we?"

Acceptable risks.

Many of us live in terror of the unknown. We tremble
at the unimagined dangers that might lie in wait for
us. We cling to the security of the familiar, unwilling
to launch into rough waters. We avoid any situation
that calls us to step outside our realm of comfort.

And so the dead-end job becomes a living mausoleum. We get trapped in unhealthy or destructive relationships because we think we can't do better or don't deserve more. We balk at the prospect of going deeper in our spiritual lives, afraid that we might uncover something that demands change.

We stay in the cove, where it's calm and safe. Risks—even acceptable risks—scare us half to death.

But life—real life, abundant, vibrant life—demands courage. The willingness to brave the stormy waters . . . to launch out beyond what we know . . . to take a chance.

So the next time you're tempted to play it safe, to stay in familiar territory where the winds don't blow and the waves don't roll, remember: It may be calmer there, but to find the fish, you have to get out of the cove.

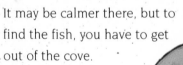

But life—real life, abundant, vibrant life—demands courage. The willingness to brave the stormy waters . . . to launch out beyond what we know . . . to take a chance.

INDEPENDENCE

"Choose your own place."

One thing I loved about fishing with my dad was that he knew all the best spots on the lake. If the fish were biting, he could find them. And he knew, too, how wind conditions, temperature, and time of day would affect the outcome of our trip. I could always count on Daddy to guide us to exactly the right place to hook into the big bass, or to locate a bream bed where they would strike at anything we cast at them.

So I couldn't have been more shocked the morning he pushed off from shore and said, "You tell me where we're going today."

I was speechless. I was supposed to decide what direction we'd take; where we'd fish? It was unthinkable. I didn't have any idea where to go. I had always depended upon him to take us where we needed to go.

Besides, what if I couldn't find the right spot? By this time I knew the way to the heavy weed beds where I'd caught my first bass. I could find the willow cove, or the rocky shore where the pine trees grew. If necessary, I could now make my way back from the other end of the lake without getting lost. But find the fish? I didn't think so.

He waited, idling the engine, until I muttered uncertainly, "Well, I guess we could go over to that bay where we caught all those bluegills a couple of weeks ago."

I watched his face for some indication of approval or disappointment, but got no sign of what he might be thinking. "Okay," he said. He revved the motor, and we started off.

That was all. Just, "Okay."

The bluegill cove turned out to be an abysmal letdown. Nothing was biting there, not even a nibble. After a while, Dad said, "Want to try somewhere else?"

I jumped at the chance.

"Yes. Where to next?"

"Your decision. You pick the spot."

I narrowed my eyes and frowned at him. "Why me?"

He shrugged. "Just thought I'd let you choose the place."

Hesitantly, I suggested the inlet where the willows grew. A bust; no action there.

Then the rocky shoreline on the south side of the lake. Nothing there, either.

By this time I was growing increasingly frustrated, both with myself and with Daddy.

"Why are you making me choose

the spots?" I asked with just a touch of anger and rebellion. "We're not catching a thing, and you know a whole lot more about where the fish are located than I do."

He looked over at me and lifted his shoulders in a shrug. "I don't know. This is not a test. We can always try something else. I just thought you might like to have a say in where we fished. You know, to pick your own place."

The balloon of anger inside me deflated. We cruised to a few more spots, finally hooked into a nice bed of bream, and went home that afternoon with a pretty respectable catch. Still, I was left with a baffling sense of dissatisfaction. Intellectually, I appreciated the fact that he let me choose. Or at least I thought I did. But somehow I couldn't help feeling as if I had been set up, deliberately forced to make decisions I wasn't equipped to make.

49

That kind of manipulation really wasn't in my father's nature, however, and not until years later did I understand my bewildering responses to what happened in the boat that day.

The revelation came when, as an adult, I was faced with one of those difficult, life-changing decisions we all encounter. I had been raised to be independent, to make my own choices. But I was also a person of faith, and I believed in Divine guidance. This particular decision had the potential of altering my course forever, and I needed the "right" answer. When I prayed for direction, I received a response deep in the recesses of my soul: *Choose your own way.* I was frustrated. I was angry. No, I was *furious.*

Here I was, a puny little human being with a severely limited sight distance, being told to choose my own way. And the Creator of the Universe, who knew what the future would hold and how important this choice

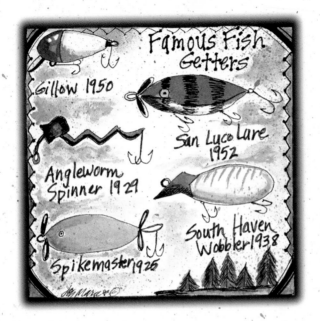

was, refused to give me any direct guidance to the right spot! I felt as if I were being tested to see how smart I was, how wise, how strong. But what if I made an incorrect decision and messed up my life forever? What if I went the wrong way? What if . . . ?

Then my mind flashed back to that day in the boat, and I heard my father's words: *"This is not a test. We can always try something else."*

In that moment, I learned a profound truth: There were no "right" or "wrong" answers in that situation. I was not being analyzed, examined, or graded—I was being given an opportunity to exercise my own free will, to have a say in where my life was going.

And I didn't need to worry if it didn't work out perfectly, because Someone Else was in the boat with me.

Someone who knew the lake better than I ever would.

Someone who cared.

Someone who loved me enough to let me choose my own place.

I was not being analyzed, examined,
or graded—I was being given an
opportunity to exercise my own
free will, to have a say in
where my life was going.

IMAGINATION

"Talk to the Fish Fairy."

Winter, such as it was in Mississippi, had come and gone. The rainy gray days had finally given way to the moment of glory that happens only once a year—the advent of spring. Almost overnight, the weather shifted. Everything blossomed all at once. And my father and I headed back to the lake.

We had been in the boat for a couple of hours, but nothing much was biting. We needed a good catch; the winter months had depleted our stock, and my mother was at home preparing side dishes for the first big fish fry of the season. To my way of thinking, this was an outrageous act of faith. Mother firmly believed that her fisherman-husband would come home with a basket full.

I felt a tug on my line and jerked to attention. "I got one!" As Daddy had taught me, I set the hook and began reeling him in. He fought valiantly, but when I got him to the surface, Dad and I both began to laugh.

It was the puniest little bluegill I had ever laid eyes on. A baby, maybe six inches long if you stretched him out on both ends. I removed the hook and prepared to release him back into the water.

"Wait a minute," Dad said. "Hand him over here."

I tossed my catch to the other end of the boat and watched as my father cradled the tiny fish in both hands. He put his mouth up to the fish's gill and began to whisper something I couldn't understand. Then, without ceremony, he slid the infant bluegill back into the water and watched as it recovered and swam away.

"What were you doing?" I asked.

He looked at me with an expression of total candor. "I was talking to the Fish Fairy."

"The Fish Fairy?"

Dad nodded solemnly. "Yep. When you catch a little one like that, you tell him to go back to the Fish Fairy and let her know what a nice person you are, putting the babies back in the lake so they'll have a chance to grow up. Then the Fish Fairy will send bigger fish along so you can catch them." He grinned.

I stared at him. My father, the down-to-earth man whose name I carried, the man who had taught me all the no-nonsense facts about fishing was now *talking to a Fish Fairy!*

I shook my head and turned back to the front of the boat without a word. But on my next cast, I hooked into a huge fat crappie, bigger than my dad's hand.

"See?" He took the fish from me and placed it in the basket that hung alongside the boat. "He'll make good eating. The Fish Fairy always comes through."

We began to catch them, one after another. Bluegills, crappie, three or four nice bass. Before long, the fish basket was bulging, with enough for dinner and some to spare.

And all because of the Fish Fairy.

Over the years my dad has developed the reputation for being a little nuts, but I have to confess that from that day on, I, too, have talked to the Fish Fairy—with surprising results. And whenever I hold a tiny fish in my hands and whisper into its gills a message for the Fish Fairy, I smile. Just the memory of it brings a lighthearted sense of joy to my heart.

57

Most of us grow out of that sense of childlike awe and mystery somewhere along the way. It's too bad. We turn away from our fantasies, abandon the magic of make-believe. We let ourselves get caught up in the stern realities of day-to-day living, in budgets and spreadsheets and Dow-Jones averages. We even take our leisure time too seriously, determined to lower our golf score or beat our opponent. Never mind having fun; we want to *win*.

My father may have been a tad eccentric, but he has left me with an enviable legacy—the ability to let my imagination spin out stories, create characters, develop scenes, grab hold of the magic in life. He has given me a heritage of wonder in the little things, a gift of spirit and heart and soul, a glorious liberty of living with abandonment and joy.

What would our lives be like, I wonder, if we learned to laugh again, to embrace the ridiculous more often, to make up silly little songs . . . to recapture our imaginations?

What if we all talked to the Fish Fairy?

What would our lives be like, I wonder, if we learned to laugh again, to embrace the ridiculous more often, to make up silly little songs?

ACCEPTANCE

"When they ain't bitin', they ain't bitin'."

One unassailable truth permeated my memories of childhood and adolescence —one foundational belief that would not be shaken:

My dad was Master of the Lake.

This wasn't just the fantasy of a little girl who adored her father. It was Truth with a capital T.

Like all fishermen, Dad swapped tales with his fishing buddies. Sometimes, I'll admit, he exaggerated

a little—that was all part of the game, and he was a wonderful storyteller. But this was no fish story. No matter what the conditions, my father always came in with the most fish in his basket. And when, in Sunday school, some teacher recounted the incident of the disciples casting their nets on the other side and pulling in a catch so large it threatened to break their nets, I understood completely. I had seen the very same thing with my own eyes.

So I couldn't comprehend what was happening that bright Saturday morning as we sat in the boat and waited.

Nothing was biting. Nothing.

We started at the weed bed. Not a nibble. Went on to the shallow cove where the willows leaned and dangled their branches among the rocks. Nothing. We cruised along the shoreline, tried every bay and inlet, even switched from live bait to artificial lures. Finally, after three hours of futility, Dad turned to me and offered a profound bit of wisdom:

"Well, honey, if they ain't bitin', they just ain't bitin'."

61

We had enough fish in the freezer, of course, to last through the next millennium. We wouldn't go hungry, wouldn't have to cancel the fish fry planned for Saturday night. But for the first time since I had begun fishing with my father, we went home empty-handed.

Gone Fishin'

62

I was discouraged. As a matter of fact, I felt like a complete failure. Then I began to notice that it didn't seem to bother Daddy very much. He took it in stride, as if it were a natural part of the process. Sometimes you win big, even bigger than your dreams. Sometimes you don't.

When they ain't bitin', they just ain't bitin'.

Many times in my adulthood that truth has resurfaced, and every time it causes me to re-evaluate my

own expectations. Is it realistic to believe that I should be the best at everything? To succeed at every new venture I try, land every job I apply for, be everyone's best friend and confidante, distinguish myself in the eyes of all?

Probably not.

Still, I've struggled over the years with wanting to be the Master of the Lake. When things didn't go the way I thought they should—when a job I wanted went to someone else, when my pet project elicited criticism rather than praise, when a relationship I valued ended up on the rocks—I found myself looking for reasons. I must have done something wrong, not been good enough, not tried hard enough. Otherwise I would have come home carrying a basket bulging with fresh fish rather than a cricket box full of unused bait.

Maybe.

63

Maybe not.

In general it's a sound principle, this habit of looking to ourselves when things go wrong. It's healthier, at least, than blaming everyone around us. But the reality is, sometimes the fish just don't bite. No matter what kind of bait we use, no matter how skilled we are, no matter how many perfect spots we try. Some days we're brilliant. Some days we're not so brilliant.

It's great to be Master of the Lake.
It's exciting to drag in a catch so
large it threatens to
swamp the boat.
But when

we've done all
we can do—when
we've cast shallow and
run deep, experimented with
every bait and lure, tried every
cove, used every skill we have at our
disposal, sometimes we just have to admit:
When they ain't bitin', they just ain't bitin'.

Is it realistic to believe that I should
be the best at everything? To succeed at
every new venture I try, land every job I apply
for, be everyone's best friend and confidante?

GRATITUDE

"Be grateful and give back."

On a typical Saturday morning, Dad would load his little pickup truck with rods and reels, gas cans, bait, tackle boxes, and whatever else we'd need for a day of fishing. But this autumn morning wasn't typical.

I climbed into the cab and craned my neck to look through the back window at the bed of the truck. In addition to the usual assortment of fishing tackle, the

truck was filled with other tools: a small chain saw, a shovel, pruning shears, rakes and hoes. "What's all this stuff?"

"You'll see."

We got to the lake, and Dad unloaded all the gear. "Aren't we going to fish?"

"Later. We've got a few other things to do first."

For an hour or more we worked—dredging out the lake bed at the waterfront, cutting down a few small evergreens. But I soon found out this wasn't just a semi-annual clean-up ritual. When we were finished at our lot, my father put the small trees we had cut into the boat and instructed me to climb in.

67

"What are we doing?"

"We're making fish houses."

I knew about birdhouses, and squirrel houses, and even bat houses. But fish houses? "Is this some kind of joke, like talking to the Fish Fairy?"

He gave me a stern look of reprimand and put his hand over his heart as if I had deeply wounded him. "Did my daughter just call the Fish Fairy a *joke*?" Then he grinned. "We're going to take these little trees and sink them underwater. They'll provide cover for the fish—a protected place for them to breed."

And so, beginning with our own frontage, we cruised slowly around the lake, submerging the evergreens into the water. I watched as my father carefully placed those newly-cut trees, creating safe havens for the fish—nurseries for the new babies that would come next spring. He gazed off into the distance for a moment, then turned back to me. "Life is a miracle," he mused, "but we have to care for it, replenish it. If we're truly grateful, we have to show it by giving something back."

What does it mean to "give back"? It means being aware of and grateful for the gifts we've been given, and being willing to share them. It means living with an open heart and an open hand, doing whatever I can, at any given time in my life, to restore the glory of the Creator's universe. It means seeing needs and meeting them without fanfare or accolades.

68

I can't do everything, but I can do something.
Something small. Something close to home.
I can create a fish house under the water's saurface.

Giving something back means
living with an open heart and an open hand.

I'll never forget the day I hooked into The Big One.

The sun was shining; the birds were singing; the fish were biting. *Really* biting. It was only two hours past sunrise, and already our fish basket was filled to overflowing. And then, just as Dad and I were about to come in, it happened.

I cast out toward the shore into a deep hole between a rock and the roots of a willow tree. I paused,

jerked the line a little, and my rod bent double. The weight of the fish nearly pulled me out of the boat.

I could feel him fighting, trying to go deeper. I maneuvered him away from the rock and the trees into open water. He began to run, thrashing, struggling to get free. And then he made for the surface, a stunning flash of silver under the water.

Even Daddy, who normally didn't get very excited, was on his feet, grabbing for the landing net, giving me instructions. "Keep your rod tip up! Give him a little line. Now, reel him in closer!"

I fought with the rod, trying to maintain control. Closer, closer ... . and then I got a glimpse of him—the biggest bass I had ever laid eyes on. He leaped from the water, thrashing from side to side, but he couldn't throw the hook. I had him. He was mine. And he was huge.

For twenty minutes I played that fish, hoping to tire him out so I could land him. But his strength matched my adrenaline, and after a while I began to wonder which one of us was the catch. Then, without warning, he stopped fighting. I reeled in carefully, praying the line wouldn't break. Dad stood by waiting with the net in the water.

I got him to the side of the boat, and now I could see clearly just how large he was. Twelve pounds, maybe fifteen, and as long as my arm. His mouth was bigger than my dad's fist.

My mind flashed to a book I had been reading for English class—Hemingway's *The Old Man and the Sea*. I hadn't been fighting this fish all night, but my muscles ached nevertheless, and just for a moment I imagined that I knew how that old man felt when he finally brought in the catch of his life.

I reached down, holding the rod aloft in my left hand and trying to hook a finger into his gill. But he was too heavy for me to lift. I coaxed him alongside the boat toward the landing net. And then, just when I thought I had him, he made a final run for freedom. The rod slipped in my grasp; the line touched the edge of the boat and snapped.

The last I saw of him was a shimmer of tail fin as he made for deep water.

I couldn't believe it. Exhausted and dumbfounded, I sat down in the front of the boat and cried.

As I recall, Daddy didn't say a word. He just waited, watching me.

What I remember saying was, "I am never going fishing again. N*ever!*"

He laughed. "Sure you will. I've lost some big ones in my time, too, you know. And I'm still fishing. You just have to learn to let go of the one that got away."

74

I have to admit that I didn't learn how to *let go* that day. Or the next. And occasionally, even now, I'm tempted to hold on to some moment from the past, to let regret and self-recrimination steal my joy in the present and my hope for the future. But when I find myself looking back, I try to remember my father's philosophical perspective on losses, big and small. You keep on fishing. You don't let yourself become obsessed with the one that got away.

Yes, the Big One got away. There's no trophy hanging on my wall, no photograph of the catch of a lifetime. But the loss doesn't diminish the thrill of trying to land him.

And I'm still fishing.

When I find myself looking back, I try
to remember my father's philosophical
perspective on losses, big and
small. You keep on fishing.

SUCCESS

"A bad day fishing is still a good day."

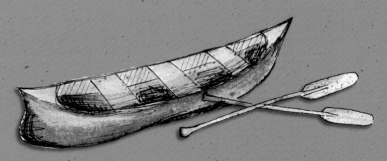

Most of the time Dad and I caught a lot of fish. A lot. One summer, we had a contest to see who could catch the most fish on a single bait. I caught three on one cricket. Daddy caught four.

But there were days, too, when the fish just weren't biting.

I remember one particular morning in early June. The air was cool, the lake as still as a mirror, reflecting back the blue of the sky and the green of the trees along the bank. It was so quiet you could hear your own heartbeat. The plop of the bait into the water sent out undisturbed ripples all the way to the bank. It was a perfect day to fish.

But apparently the fish didn't know how perfect the day was.

We got, in my father's words, "nary a nibble."

We tried everywhere. But even our best spots came up empty. It was as if some diabolical villain had come in the night and spirited all the fish away.

Dad didn't seem to be the least bit ruffled. He leaned back against the outboard motor, cast leisurely this way and that, talked to the ducks as they paddled by, poured a cup of coffee from his thermos.

Finally I couldn't stand it any longer. "Doesn't it bother you, not catching anything?" I asked.

He reeled in slowly, shrugged, and smiled at me. "It happens. Sometimes they're biting, and sometimes they're not."

I had heard this before, of course, but I didn't like it any better for the repetition.

77

"Look around," he went on. "It's a beautiful day. We're out here, relaxing on the lake. The sun is shining, and I'm with my favorite daughter." He adjusted his hat and peered at me under the brim. "A bad day fishing is still a good day."

I thought about it for a moment, and in spite of myself, I had to agree with him. What was really important was not the size of the catch, but the time I was spending with my father.

We stayed a couple more hours, drifting here and there, talking. We laughed together at the funny, awkward ducklings who paddled across the lake in a wobbly line, struggling to keep up with their parents. We reflected on the beauty all around us, and how the magnificence of creation testifies to the presence of a Creator. We shared fond memories of the past and visions for the future.

We went home that day without a single bite. But although the fish basket might have been empty, my soul was filled to overflowing. Just from spending time with my father.

78

What was really important was not
the size of the catch, but the time
I was spending with my father.

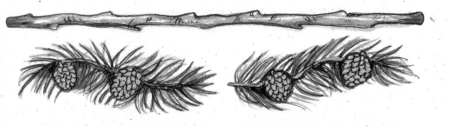

PATIENCE

"Patience, patience."

When I was in my twenties, I had the pleasure of re-living the memories of some of those early fishing trips with my father. My niece Marti, Daddy's only granddaughter, was four or five when we took her to the lake for the first time. Her mother had warned us sternly, "Don't go taking her out in that little boat. She's too young."

And so we stood on a neighbor's dock and fixed her up with a cane pole and bright red bobber—the very same pole, I firmly believed, that I had used during my Opie Taylor days.

Marti, of course, was much smaller than I had been on my first fishing trip with Dad, so the "bait your own hook, clean your own catch" law was waived for her. Dad threaded a cricket onto her hook and knelt down beside her, looking her solemnly in the eye.

"Now Martha," he said sternly, "there are some rules in fishing. The first rule is that you have to be patient."

She puckered up her forehead in an imitation of his frown and repeated, "Patient."

"Yes. Do you know what patience means?"

She thought about this for a minute, then nodded firmly. "It's like when Mommy takes me to the mall, and we go to the shoe store and the clothes place first, and the toy store after. It means I gotta wait."

Daddy grinned up at me. "That's right," he told her. "If you want to fish, you have to be patient and wait for the fish to come. And the second rule is, you have to be quiet so you won't scare the fish away. Can you do that?"

Marti put her finger over her lips. "Yes, Pa Jim. Quiet."

"All right. Let's get your line in the water." He dropped her bait over the side of the dock and handed her the pole. "Watch the red bobber. If it bounces up and down in the water, it means you've got a fish."

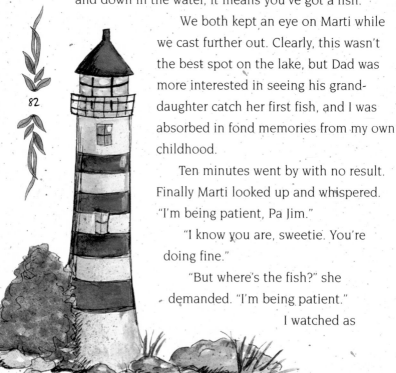

We both kept an eye on Marti while we cast further out. Clearly, this wasn't the best spot on the lake, but Dad was more interested in seeing his granddaughter catch her first fish, and I was absorbed in fond memories from my own childhood.

Ten minutes went by with no result. Finally Marti looked up and whispered. "I'm being patient, Pa Jim."

"I know you are, sweetie. You're doing fine."

"But where's the fish?" she demanded. "I'm being patient."

I watched as

82

Daddy fought hard to suppress his laughter. "Give it a little more time, honey."

She waited, growing more antsy by the second. Then, at last, a tiny nibble pulled her bobber under. "Pa Jim!" she yelled, forgetting all about the quiet rule. "Pa Jim! I got a fish!"

Dad dropped his pole and went over to help her. Sure enough, a little crappie had taken her bait and was firmly lodged on the hook. "Hold on tight," he instructed, "and pull up—very gently."

Marti yanked the pole up with all her four-year-old might, and the little fish came flying out of the water and slapped down on the dock behind her.

She ran over to survey her trophy while Dad took it off the hook and placed it gently in a five-gallon tub of water. The tiny little fellow righted himself and swam around in the bucket.

"I was patient, Pa Jim!" Marti squealed at the top of her lungs. "I was *patient*!"

Once we got home, everyone oohed and ahhed over Marti's pint-sized fish.

Despite the fact that it was worth only one or two bites, Daddy cleaned it and cooked it with the rest of the mess and served it to Marti with a flourish. She never said, "I caught one!" Instead, she bragged proudly, "I was patient!"

84

For months after that first fishing trip with Marti, her words became the standard line in our family for anything that merited celebration. Not "I caught a twelve-pound bass," or "I was promoted today," or "I got a scholarship to grad school," but "I was patient." And considering the fact that most good things in life come through patience, it wasn't an idle boast.

Perhaps we'd all be wiser if our life's goal was not to be successful or smart or wealthy or admired, but to be *patient*. And then, when good things come—when we discover the love of a lifetime, see a dream come to fulfillment, or accomplish an ambition for which we've worked for years—we can hold up that catch with pride and say, "I was patient."

Patience, and the mulberry leaf

becomes a silk gown.

CHINESE PROVERB

VULNERABILITY

"What do you think I should do?"

When I was a little girl, Saturday mornings on the lake became a refuge for me, a place where I could spend uninterrupted time with Dad. Like most children, I gave little thought to the stresses and problems that tugged at my father's mind and heart. I perceived him as invincible, strong, wise, funny . . . pretty close to perfect.

As I grew to adulthood, I learned—theoretically,

Vulnerability

anyway—that parents are simply people, people with anxieties and conflicts and dilemmas just like the rest of us. And one particular Saturday morning I got an unaccustomed glimpse into my father's heart.

I came to visit my parents during a break in my grad school schedule, and as I look back on that time, I was probably caught up in the myriad of problems that absorbed my attention—choosing a topic for my dissertation, preparing for oral exams, obsessing about a job after graduation. I'm sure I spent most of our time over dinner Friday night talking about myself. But when Dad asked if I'd like to go fishing the next morning, I jumped at the chance.

Being on the lake with him brought back the best memories of my childhood, that familiar and welcome sense of being at home within myself, of all being right with the world. My concerns seemed a thousand miles away as I gazed over the serenity of the lake and cast into a glassy calm.

Then I noticed that Daddy wasn't saying much. He seemed distracted, as if he had something weighing on his mind.

"It's a beautiful morning, isn't it?" I ventured.

"Yes."

"Is everything okay, Dad?"

He turned to me. "Why do you ask?"

"I don't know." I hesitated, not wanting to pry. "You just seem . . . well, distracted."

"The lake is a good place to sort things out," he mused. "You cast, you reel, you wait. Your mind is left free to think."

88

"Anything in particular you need to sort out?"

Much to my surprise, he laid down his rod, poured a cup of coffee for each of us, and began to talk. And for the first time in my memory, he spoke not as a father talking to his daughter, but as friend to friend, equal to equal.

Dad had long been an elder in the church. But there were problems with the new pastor, changes that made him question whether he was in the right place. He and Mother no longer felt as if they were getting any spiritual nourishment from the services. "I've talked with the pastor and with the other elders," he concluded, "but it doesn't look as if the situation's likely to improve. Your mother and I are considering changing churches. What do *you* think I should do?"

I sat there, dumbfounded, as the significance of the question sank into my mind: My father was asking *my* advice about a spiritual matter! I felt awed and humbled. And I knew that in that critical moment our relationship had moved into a new dimension.

I barely recall my answer. Something about following his heart, finding a place where his soul could be fed and nurtured. What I do remember was my father's candor, his vulnerability, his willingness to bare his soul at a critical time in his life.

I caught a glimpse, that morning on the lake with Dad, of the power of vulnerability. When he bared his soul, asked his question, sought my advice,

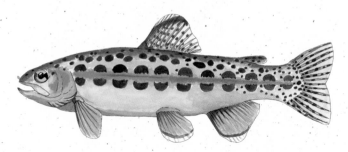

he changed my perception of him forever. I still see my father as strong and wise and funny, but no longer invincible. No longer perfect.

90

But it wasn't a loss; it was a transformation. He didn't lose face by allowing me into that hidden place where his most profound doubts and questions lay. He didn't undermine my respect for him by revealing his weaknesses and struggles.

Instead, he gave me a great gift. He invited me to be a participant in a significant change point in his life. He honored me by trusting me with his concerns, by valuing my perspectives.

And he did it with a single question: "What do *you* think I should do?"

I still see my father as strong

and wise and funny, but

no longer invincible.

INNER PEACE

"When it's hot, the fish go deep."

It was a sweltering summer morning, the temperatures already climbing toward the nineties. A haze of humidity hung in the air, and even breathing felt like work.

Still, it was a good day to get a tan—or in my case, a sizzling burn. In a tank top and cut-offs, I hung my bare feet over the side of the boat and tried to dangle them in the water. But I was too short to reach, and

after a few minutes I put my tennis shoes back on. Heat rose off the metal plating of the boat in waves.

Dad threw a baseball cap in my direction—a welcome relief from the sun. "Let's go someplace shady," I suggested.

"Not if you want to catch any fish." He shook his head. "When it's hot, the fish go deep."

So out we went in the blazing sun to the center of the lake, where the deep holes were. Once we had anchored, he flipped on his handy-dandy sonic fish finder and motioned me over to peer into the little screen. There, in a blurred image, I saw them. Far down below us, resting in the cool reaches of the deeper water.

93

We brought in a few nice ones, but I have to admit I didn't last long that day. The heat was just too intense. By the time we returned to the comfort of a cold shower and an air-conditioned house, my shoulders were blistered and my head was throbbing. Still, I learned an important principle from Dad and Mother Nature that day—a lesson I've applied over and over again in my adult life:

When it gets hot, go deep.

Life has a way of turning up the burners from time to time. Decisions, choices, family struggles, job stresses, relationship breakdowns, financial troubles, health crises. The heat rises, so intense that we can barely breathe. The walls close in, we can find no way out.

That's when it's time to go deep. Down below the noises that confuse our minds, beneath the surface fires that threaten to shrivel our spirits and drain our souls. There, in the depths of the heart, we find the inner peace that cannot be shaken by circumstance.

94

Going deep is not an escape, nor is it an easy answer to life's difficult questions. It's not the end of the search, but the place of beginning again. When we look into ourselves, into the inmost places of our souls, into our relationship with God and with one another, we find the trust and the courage and the fortitude to face life's challenges. We find the faith to believe through our present situation.

No, we can't prevent the heat from rising. But we can go deep.

In the depths of the heart, we find the
inner peace that cannot be shaken
by circumstance.

☆ CONTENTMENT ☆

"Sufficient unto the day is the catch thereof."

Because Daddy and I fished on a private lake, there were no limits on the number of fish we could take home. In those days there weren't any catch-and-release laws—except the ones Dad imposed upon himself in his dealings with the Fish Fairy. So it wasn't uncommon that we would go to lake at sunrise and leave at noon with fifty or sixty nice bluegills.

Contentment

One morning, however, the rules changed.

We had found a great spot, a bream bed where everything was biting. We hadn't moved the boat in two hours—just sat there, pulling them in one after another. Between us, we threw back twenty or so small ones, and still the keepers were filling the fish basket. I didn't have to be patient that day—nearly every time I cast, I came up with a strike. And I was having a wonderful time!

Then, out of the blue, Daddy lifted the fish basket out of the water and eyed our catch. "I think it's about time to go," he said.

97

"Go? Now?" I couldn't believe it. "But they're biting like crazy. You could practically put a naked hook out there and catch something."

"Yes, but we're not having company tonight, and your brother won't be home for dinner. It'll just be the three of us. We've got enough." He grinned. "Sufficient unto the day is the catch thereof."

To my young mind, that line of reasoning didn't make a bit of sense. Why leave when there are more fish to catch? We might never have another day as good as this one.

Thanks, Dad!

But to my father, it was perfectly logical. He wasn't interested in breaking records or bragging about how many fish he caught on any given day. We had *enough*, and he was content.

By contrast, the world around us insists that enough is never enough. It encourages us to want more . . . and more . . . and more. But most of us, if we're really honest, would have to admit that we have enough—more than enough.

Something miraculous happens when we finally realize that enough is enough. We start being grateful for what we have rather than concerned about what we don't have. We begin to acknowledge a Power beyond ourselves as the source of our sufficiency. We find new eyes to look not above ourselves at those who set the standard of wealth, but around us, to those who have needs. And we discover that our excess can be a source of blessing to those who have less than we do.

Enough is enough.

I'm learning to leave the lake while the fish are still biting.

Something miraculous happens when
we finally realize that enough is enough.
We start being grateful for what we
have rather than concerned
about what we don't have.

EXPLORATION

"Keep casting until you find your spot."

All through my childhood and youth, and even into my college years, Daddy and I fished together. As I grew older, our trips to the lake weren't so frequent any more, but I cherished our time together nevertheless. In the boat, somehow, we both seemed more relaxed, more at ease with ourselves and each other. We could talk about important things, or we didn't have to talk at all.

One spring weekend during graduate school I came home for a visit, and on Saturday morning the sun rose on the two of us in the boat, drinking coffee and casting into a favorite spot.

"What do you plan to do this summer?" Dad asked after a while.

I shrugged. I had been supporting myself and paying for graduate school by teaching classes at the University, but I was mentally exhausted and emotionally burned out. "I don't know. I might be able to teach a class or two during the summer session—enough to pay the rent, anyway."

He looked over at me. "You seem tired, honey."

"I'm worn out," I admitted. "I've taught three classes every semester, in addition to taking courses and planning my dissertation. I don't really want to teach this summer, but what choice do I have?"

He gave me an inscrutable expression. "If you didn't have to worry about money this summer, what would you do?"

I knew the answer immediately. "I'd stay in my apartment and write. Not my dissertation, like I *should*,

101

but poetry and short stories. Stuff just for me. I really think I'd like to become a writer, Dad. But everybody keeps telling me I can't possibly make a living at it. Still, I'd like to give it a shot. One of my professors has agreed to do some mentoring for me. She knows what's good and what's not, and she can tell me whether or not I have a chance to make it."

He thought about that for a minute. "Well, your mother and I have been talking. If you'll accept it, we've decided to pay your rent this summer so you can be free to do the writing you want to do."

I stared at him. My parents had paid for undergraduate school, but I had worked my way through two graduate programs on my own. "Are you serious?"

"Yes."

"But Daddy, you don't understand. Probably nothing I write this summer will ever be published, ever earn a dime. It's just an experiment—a dream. It's not the least bit practical."

He smiled and threw his line out into the lake. "Sometimes being impractical is important. We need to be able to follow our dreams. It's like fishing. You cast here, and if that doesn't work, you try over there. But you keep casting until you find your spot."

He reeled in, re-baited, and watched me for a minute. "Don't let go of your dreams, honey. Keep at it.

Explore. You'll find your spot. And if one summer of free rent helps you do that, it's well worth the price."

The price came to a total of about five hundred dollars, but for me it was a gift worth millions. I spent that summer writing, reading, learning, talking with my professor about my dreams and ambitions and goals. It wasn't the end of the journey, by any means, but it was a beginning. I discovered my passion.

Exploration is a scary prospect for most of us. It's

Thanks, Dad!

easier to take the safe road, to follow the well-marked path, to concede to the line of least resistance. From the cradle we're trained to be practical, to use our heads, to avoid risking the security of the familiar. But sometimes it's important to be impractical, to follow our hearts and take a chance.

Dreaming feeds our souls. And whatever our cherished hopes or secret longings, they've been given to us for a reason. They spur us onward toward experiences we have not yet known. They stretch us, enlarge our horizons, bring us joy, teach us faith. And when we honor them by exploring the undiscovered possibilities, sometimes they lead us to a fulfillment greater than anything we've ever dreamed of.

If we can just keep casting until we find our spot.

Dreaming feeds our souls. And whatever
our cherished hopes or secret longings,
they've been given to us for a reason.

GOD CONSCIOUSNESS

"Wherever you are, God is."

When my father wasn't hooking into the Big One or talking to the Fish Fairy or building nurseries for next spring's babies, I often caught him meditating. Just staring out over the lake, watching the way the breeze stirred up diamond-studded reflections on the waves, listening to the sounds of the wind in the pines.

I know this because once, when I was a teenager, I asked him.

"Whatcha doing, Daddy?"

He smiled, his faraway look vanishing as he gazed at me. "Just eavesdropping."

"You hear something?" I strained to listen, but my inexperienced ears heard nothing but silence.

"You know," he mused, "we go to church every Sunday. Sit in the second row, sing the hymns, repeat the liturgy, listen to the sermon. And that's important, don't get me wrong. But most of the time I feel closer to God out here on the lake than I do inside a church building."

I thought about that for a minute. I liked church, which of course made me an irredeemable geek in the eyes of my peers. I even enjoyed confirmation class. But something in my father's words stirred a new awarness in me—an understanding I had never found words for.

"Wherever you are, God is," he went on. "You can't escape it, not if you have your eyes and ears open."

He fell silent, and we went back to fishing. My dad wasn't one to talk much about his faith or to impose it on others, and he certainly didn't consider himself a theologian. But in that brief moment he imparted to me a glimmer of spiritual insight that helped shape my own relationship with the Almighty.

Worship is about perception, not about precepts. It's about being *God-conscious*, having eyes and ears open to the presence of the Almighty in unexpected places. It doesn't just happen in a cathedral or a temple, on a Sunday morning or a Sabbath. Worship happens anywhere, any time, when the curtains of our mundane lives part to give us a glimpse of the glory beyond ourselves.

Wherever you are, God is.

Worship happens anywhere, any
time, when the curtains of our mundane
lives part to give us a glimpse of
the glory beyond ourselves.

OPTIMISM

"It's going to be a good day."

By nature, I'm not a morning person. I like to sleep late, rise leisurely, and not rush into anything before I absolutely have to. But if I wanted to go fishing with Daddy, I had to get up early—at least on Saturdays. I had to drag myself out of bed and get dressed, tiptoe around the house so as not to wake Mother, and be in the truck ready to go when Dad pulled out of the driveway—before sunrise!

Daddy, bless his heart, had the sensitivity not to try to carry on a conversation with me before I was fully awake. But I do remember one thing he said, regular as clockwork, every Saturday morning. He would walk out into the chilly pre-dawn, squint at the sky, and murmur with a contented sigh, "It's going to be a good day."

I didn't think much of it at the time. He loved to fish, and to him, any day on the lake was "a good day." But as I grew older, I began to realize that this wasn't just his philosophy about fishing. It was a perspective of optimism that permeated almost everything he did.

Daddy didn't much believe in wasting time and energy on negative attitudes. He couldn't tolerate whining, and he taught me, both by precept and example, to give myself fully to whatever I chose to do, and to look forward to tomorrow.

That morning, when my father stood in the driveway squinting at the clouds and declaring that it was going to be a good day, he had no way of *knowing* what the day would bring. He couldn't see into the future. He simply trusted, and embraced the unknown with

confidence. He was an optimist, and I was the optimist's daughter.

That's probably why I grew up with the conviction that the future presented a thrilling array of limitless possibilities. That whatever I set my mind to, I could accomplish. My mind and heart were filled with the anticipation of new challenges and adventures, and my only fear of tomorrow was the fear of missing out on an exciting opportunity.

Perspective helps determine what the future will hold. It's not so much a matter of *what* happens, but of *how* I perceive it. Optimism turns failure into hope; pessimism transforms success into dread.

We can never know what tomorrow will bring.

But for now, it's going to be good day.

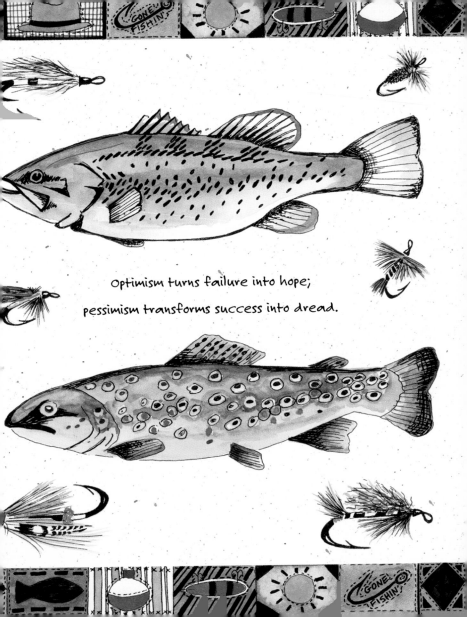

Optimism turns failure into hope;

pessimism transforms success into dread.

Character is formed on a deeper level,
a reflection of the images that pervade
and inform our lives when we are
least conscious of them.